ideals CHRISTMAS

This wonderful season of the year,
In Christmas spirit bound,
Imparts the glow of Yuletide cheer
Expressed in joyous sound.

This happy time for young and old
Amid the frosted scene,
Gone the tints of autumn gold,
Gather now the evergreen.

Holly, mistletoe and berry
Adorn the festive board,
And wide-eyed children, laughing, merry,
Await the birthday of our Lord.

Greetings then to all mankind,
Beloved of Jesus from His birth,
May you in peace and friendship find
Enjoyment of this blessed earth.

Throughout this season of good will
Let true love point the way
And into every heart instill
The magic that is Christmas Day.
MERRY CHRISTMAS!

Victor G. C. Norwood

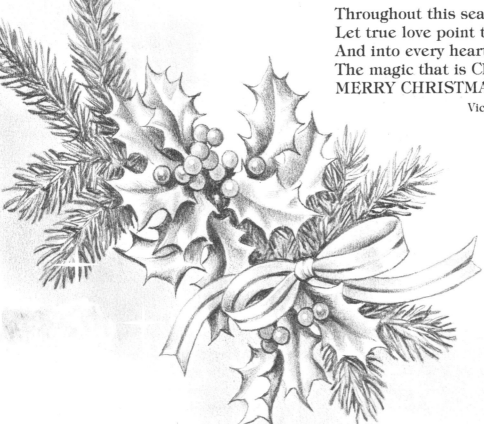

ISBN 0-8249-1015-X 350

IDEALS—Vol. 39, No. 8 December MCMLXXXII IDEALS (ISSN 0019-137X) is published eight times a year,
February, March, April, June, August, September, November, December
by IDEALS PUBLISHING CORPORATION, 11315 Watertown Plank Road, Milwaukee, Wis. 53226
Second class postage paid at Milwaukee, Wisconsin. Copyright © MCMLXXXII by IDEALS PUBLISHING CORPORATION.
POSTMASTER: Send address changes to Ideals, Post Office Box 2100, Milwaukee, Wis. 53201
All rights reserved. Title IDEALS registered U.S. Patent Office.
Published simultaneously in Canada.

ONE YEAR SUBSCRIPTION—eight consecutive issues as published—$15.95
TWO YEAR SUBSCRIPTION—sixteen consecutive issues as published—$27.95
SINGLE ISSUE—$3.50

Publisher, James A. Kuse
Editor/Ideals, Colleen Callahan Gonring
Associate Editor, Linda Robinson
Production Manager, Mark Brunner
Photographic Editor, Gerald Koser
Copy Editor, Barbara Nevid
Art Editor, Duane Weaver

The Magic of Christmas

Cynthia Holt Cummings

I'm counting the days until Christmas;
I'm watching the skies fall down
With snowflakes that come so gently
To cover the earth of brown.

I'm wrapping the gifts of Christmas
With love and joy in my heart,
And I'm ending the year with magic
To give the New Year a start.

The trees that are tall and stately
In their winter coats of green
Will soon wear the colors of Christmas,
Become part of the Christmas scene.

Lights will be blinking;
Bells will be ringing;
Voices will echo with song.
Oh, for the magic of Christmas
To last the whole year long!

A German Christmas

Martin Hintz

Feathery snow, gaily decorated trees, ornate creches, jingling sleigh bells, brilliant night-time skies, flickering candles, soaring carols—these are the Yule gifts that Germany awaits each year. There are few other countries anywhere that are so Christmas conscious. West Germany is an expansive sprawl of Alps and Black Forest, of seacoast and inland lakes, of meadows and rolling hills that has enough Christmas traditions per mile to fill a fleet of Santa's sleighs.

The country celebrates Christmas with a capital C. It has been this way for untold generations, since the first hardy missionaries ventured into the Teutonic wilderness, bringing the message of Christ's peace and love. War, famine, depression, and political turmoil have not been able to shake the German love affair with this most holy of holidays. The Germans have subsequently been more than willing to share their delightful exuberance with the rest of the world, and we've all been the better for it.

The excitement begins even as the first autumn leaves turn golden brown and drift to the ground, carpeting the landscape with their crunchy feel underfoot. The upbeat holiday feeling continues for months.

Germans build up to Christmas gradually, starting their celebration on Saint Martin's Day, the eleventh of November. This feast day honors a Roman soldier who shared his cloak with a shivering beggar. The impoverished man was actually the disguised Christ according to the wonderful legend. The tradition of gift giving, as exemplified by the concerned saint, has continued to this day, much to the delight of youngsters who are the principal beneficiaries of all the góodies. On that day, as well, in the regions of Eifel, Sauerland, Theingau, and Westerwald, children carry lanterns and torches through the winding village streets. At night, high on the hills over the towns, they will light the Martinmas fires; the blazes, signifying light and hope in the advent of winter, can be seen for miles.

Next comes Saint Nicholas Day on the sixth of December, another holiday expressly for children who again receive gifts of fruit and candy. From the Saint Nicholas character, which probably stems from a medieval king figure, we in the United States get our own Santa Claus with his white beard and elaborate red costume. The German Nicholas rides about on a great white horse, followed by his grimy and grumpy manservant who usually goes by the name of Ruprecht. This character hands out gifts to the good youngsters and punishes the bad ones, including—supposedly—dipping them into a giant inkpot!

But anyone who travels through Germany in early December hoping to meet the good Saint Nicholas might be in for a surprise, especially in eastern sections of the country. The Ashman in Pomerania, the Shaggy Goat of West Prussia, and the East Prussian Bag of Bones are based in pagan lore. They ask for gifts for themselves, displaying very little Christian charity. The figures are dressed in animal skins and straw, designed to scare the little ones.

The annual Christmas market opens early in December, offering for sale almost every imaginable holiday item from candles to candy. Many town centers are crammed with tiny stalls displaying oodles of decorations, trees, baked goods, and similar delights. If you can't find a present here, you just haven't looked long enough! Youngsters love wandering from booth to booth in these Christmas fairs or "Christ Child markets," as they are sometimes called. Munich's market dates from the 1300s, while the one in Bonn is barely two decades old. Regardless of the history of a Christmas fair in a specific city, the popularity of the event is undeniable.

As the time gets closer to Christmas, the weather turns colder. The markets become quiet, almost hushed, as the vendors huddle over their tiny coal-fed fires. Last-minute shoppers are the same anywhere as they rush around stocking up on wares.

For the child who plans ahead, a list of wishes is a must. Children's notes are often addressed to Father Christmas or to the Christ Child and are gaily decorated with bright illustrations. The feeling is that the better the drawings, the more gifts are forthcoming. Some youngsters even sprinkle sugar on the letter, just to be sure that the holy recipient knows that the sender has been good for that preceding year. Himmelreich (Kingdom of Heaven) in northern Germany is always inundated with letters for weeks before Christmas. Children seem to think the town's postal service has a direct line upwards where such an important letter really counts.

All the stores close promptly at one in the afternoon on Christmas Eve as everyone hurries home to put on their best clothes and sit down to a magnificent supper. While the children are eating, the parents slip the presents under the tree in the front room.

As soon as the first church bells sound the call to Vespers, an evening prayer service in the Catholic districts of Germany, the head of the house rings a tiny bell to tell everyone that Father Christmas has arrived. The youngest child has the lucky duty of opening the door to the room with all the presents. The resulting scene as everyone crowds around the tree is best left to the imagination!

Even with all the gift giving and the huge meals, the true spirit of Christmas is never forgotten. Both Catholic and Protestant faiths offer midnight services in the country's great cathedrals and tiny village churches. The sounds of carols flow over the wintry countryside as easily as new-fallen snow. Everything is awash with light because many parishioners bring their own candles and lanterns to church. It is traditional to keep silent on the way to the Christmas liturgy, but once the services are over, everyone explodes with holiday greetings.

Then it's home to bed and dreams of toys and sugarplums. Festive meals round out Christmas Day, and more gifts are exchanged as relatives and friends drop by to say hello and offer holiday greetings.

In the center of all this hubbub stands the Christmas tree, one of the best exports that Germany had for the rest of us. Candles are still used to decorate the silver or blue spruce that seems to be most popular. Giant firs stand outside public buildings, decorated by means of firemen's ladders. Offices and homes seem to outdo each other with their decorations. In several places, living trees are given the honor of being the community's official Yule tree.

So from gift giving to marzipan to beautiful carols, Germany has long given treasured customs to the rest of the world. Even after a full and happy Christmas Day, the festivities don't end. There's Saint Stephen's Day to celebrate on the twenty-sixth of December, leading into the Holy Twelve Nights that extend to Epiphany, the Feast of the Three Kings, on the sixth of January.

Germans simply don't want Christmas to slip away from them, but as the days grow longer and the late winter melts into spring, they eventually turn their thoughts to other holidays. Always, in the back of their minds, however, are the dreams of the next year's Christmas.

The Lovely Things of Christmas

I love the sights of Christmas.

Candles glowing through windows, sparkly-clean,
Doorways framed in holly and fragrant evergreen,
A Yule log burning on an open hearth,
Twinkly-bright stars shining over the earth,
Brightly wrapped packages neath a lovely tree,
Children as good as children can be—
I love the sights of Christmas.

I love the sounds of Christmas.

Skaters skimming over ice that's crystal clear,
Sweet carol voices on the still night air,
Footsteps squeaking on crunchy snow,
Joyous laughter where the children go,
Church bells ringing from a steeple high,
Friendly greetings to each passerby,
The jingling and tinkling of bobsled bells
Mingling gaily with the sledders' yells—
I love the sounds of Christmas.

I love the story of Christmas.

The angels' sweet message—let me hear it again—
Of peace on earth, good will toward all men;
How the shepherds made haste and, forsaking their sheep,
Found the lowly manger and the Baby, asleep.
Brave Wise Men traveled from the East afar
To worship the Babe, having followed the star;
Costly gifts at His feet they laid,
The King of all kings who was born that day.
I love the story of Christmas.

Mrs. Paul E. King

Alice Kennelly Roberts

Alice Kennelly Roberts began writing at the age of twelve and published many of her early poems while she was in high school and college. She was born and grew up in Covington, Kentucky, and attended Eastern Kentucky University where she received a degree in education. She later graduated cum laude from Cornell University with a MA in journalism and began working toward a PhD at Harvard University. She has taught all age levels, from elementary to college, and is presently a counselor and scholarship coordinator at Oak Hills High School in suburban Cincinnati. Three books of her poetry have been published: *Bluegrass, Bluegrass Junior,* and *Bluegrass Seasons.* In 1953, Mrs. Roberts began writing for Ideals. From 1954 to 1981, she wrote a daily poetry column, *Rime 'n' Reason,* for The Cincinnati Enquirer. Mrs. Roberts and her husband, Edward, have traveled around the world and are active in civic and social groups.

The Heart of Christmas

Have you been to the Land of Christmas
Where the firs and hemlocks grow,
Where their tips are lost in the stardust
And their boughs are tinseled with snow?

Have you shared in the dream of Christmas
With starry-eyed girls and boys
Who trust that a jolly Santa
Will answer their note—with toys?

Have you dwelt in the glow of Christmas,
The candles glimmering far,
A chorus of angel voices,
And light from a distant star?

Have you felt all the love of Christmas
In friendship with those who care?
Then you've peeped in the heart of Christmas,
And the Christ Child Himself is there!

The Star of Christmas

The stars have always challenged man
To look beyond the earth
For something higher than himself—
Ideals of greater worth.

And so it was, God chose a Star
To point the heavenward way,
To tell the story of His Son
On that first Christmas Day.

It brought a light to all the world,
To every lonely part,
And left a universe of hope
Within each human heart.

Today we clasp that universe;
Our orbits circle far,
Yet still unequaled and unmatched—
God's lovely Christmas Star!

Christmas Windows

There are dreams in Christmas windows,
Symbols of love and joy,
And hopes of happy childhood
For some little girl or boy.

There's a vision of chubby fingers
And arms reaching out to hold,
A smile that is wreathed in dimples,
Surpassing its worth in gold.

Yes, dreams are in Christmas windows,
But the giver himself must share,
Must join in the love of giving,
Or the gift becomes plain and bare.

And so, as the snowflakes glisten
In our Christmas world apart,
The dreams in a bright shop window
Are Christmas in someone's heart!

Christmas Reflections

The heart is filled with memories
As Christmastime draws near,
And in each festive ornament,
Some cherished scenes appear.

They hang in fragile brilliance there,
Suspended on the tree,
Tied to the past with ribboned bows,
Blest scenes that used to be—

The snow piled high on fence and post,
A steeple gainst the sky,
The moon, church windows warm with light,
The Christ Child's tiny cry.

Yes, ornaments are breakable,
But deep within the heart,
The scene we love, reflected here,
Will never quite depart.

Christmastime

Christmastime's for dreaming
Thoughts of long ago,
Holidays of childhood,
Memories all aglow.

Christmastime's for music,
Carols and angel choirs,
Hymns from snow-capped steeples,
Glowing ember's fires.

Christmastime's for loving
Friends and kindred, too,
All the weak and friendless,
All the tried and true.

Christmastime's for praying
That our hearts may see
Over stars and candles
To eternity!

A Christmas Nose

You can tell it's Christmas by carols and bells,
But Christmas also has beautiful smells.
Ginger, brown in the cookie pan,
Sends out word of the gingerbread man.
Cardamom, nutmeg, cloves and mace
Waft in clouds all over the place.
There's sage for dressing and chestnuts popping
And lovely vanilla and almond topping
For little cakes and, of course, mince pies
With scents so strong it waters the eyes,
And wax on the floors and polish on handles
And wintry fragrance of bayberry candles.
But the very best Christmas smell there'll be
Is the mountain green of the Christmas tree.

Virginia Brasier

Christmas

Christmas is a very special time of the year for friends and relatives and hearth-warmed reunions. Home becomes the focal point during this intimate celebration. Home is a traditionally trimmed, gift-wrapped place.

As the nights lengthen and the wintry winds arrive and the outdoors turns cripsy cold, the inside radiates warmth from a blazing fire. The kitchen fills with sugary smells, and the rooms are illuminated by multicolored lights of merriment.

A beautifully grown, freshly cut evergreen stands majestically. The aroma of the forest saturates the home; the perfume of pine permeates the farthest corner. Upon the top of this Christmas tree, a star is placed.

The branches of the tree open wide to welcome its ornaments: a little blue bird from Aunt Martha, a slightly ragged cloth candy cane made by a child some years ago, brightly colored balls—new—replacing the ones the cat had friskily pawed, and the shimmering icicles placed with such deliberate care.

The manger is dusted, the sweet faces of Christmas are tenderly wiped of their summer slumber, and under this most beautiful of trees, the story of Christmas is arranged—like last year, like next year.

Out come the Christmas stockings, of deepest red trimmed with slightly yellowed white cuffs of a childhood. Anxiously the stockings are hung with nails carefully placed in last year's holes. The little green elf appears in the most unlikely place, hopping about, the jester of the season.

Dishes filled with candy tidbits, nuts, and fruit and plates of patterned cookies abound to tempt the appetite. Packages spirited from underneath beds, from on top of closet shelves, from inside dresser drawers tempt the imagination. A plump turkey wrapped in brown paper in the freezer awaits the cranberries and the chestnut dressing.

On the front door of the home, a wreath laced with snowflakes and a large red ribbon gives a clue to what awaits inside. The porch light casts a soft glow upon the newly fallen snow; a bell rings inside the house.

Home, traditionally trimmed for this Christmas season, opens its door and welcomes the traveler. Christmas is the season for visiting and sharing and remembering. The remembrance of home remains throughout the year to be refurbished again another season.

Judith Lane

Christmas Loves

I wrap each gift most carefully,
And with bright ribbons tied,
I think of all good things you've done
And seal my love inside.

Gifts may be large or very small,
But each is wrapped with pride,
And with good wishes from the heart
I seal my love inside.

It is good to give and to receive
From loved ones true and tried,
And as I wrap, I meditate
And seal my love inside.

The given gift may soon wear out,
But this one thing truly abides—
It's just to know you are dear to me
As I seal my love inside.

Mamie Ozburn Odum

Poinsettias

We hail you, lovely Christmas Flower,
  With scarlet petals bright;
How gracefully you bear your name,
  The Flower of Holy Night!

Your beauty takes the breath away—
  In fields of brilliant blooms,
In gaily planted garden plots,
  In quiet living rooms.

But most of all in every church,
  With chancel all aglow,
You thrill the hearts of worshipers
And wondrous beauty show.

You symbolize for all of us
  The hopes of Christmas Day;
You decorate our gifts of love
  And brighten all our way.

Repeat the message that we need,
  Dear Flower of Holy Night;
Remind us of the Savior's love
  And keep us in His light.

J. Harold Gwynne, D.D.

Holly Fairies

Oh, fairies love a holly tree—
The foliage makes a roof
of sturdy shingles,
always green
and new and weatherproof.

And even under winter skies
the berries burn so bright
they look like
little fairy lamps
with bulbs of crimson light.

Oh, fairies love a holly spray
too much by far to leave,
and so they up and follow it
indoors on Christmas Eve.

And that is why each house
is blessed
where holly sprigs are seen,
because the fairies
still are there
beneath the red and green.

Aileen Fisher

Reprinted from CHRISTMAS PLAYS AND PROGRAMS by Aileen Fisher.
Copyright © 1960, 1970 by Aileen Fisher. Plays, Inc., Publishers, Boston, MA.

The Orphan and the Christmas Tree

Edward C. Colwell

I'd like to tell a story as it was told to me
Of a child who had no parents, and a lonely Christmas tree.
The little tree stood on a hill, not very far from here,
And pined away the hours, for no other trees were near.

The playful wind, to cheer it, would do the very best,
And in its boughs, some blue jays once tried to build a nest.
But still its deep-felt sorrow it seemed would never end,
For there alone upon the hill, it didn't have a friend.

One day a little orphan came walking up the hill.
From somewhere in the valley, the wind was sharp and chill.
He stopped beside the Christmas tree, a tear rolled down his cheek,
And through the pain of sorrow said, "If you could only speak,

"I'd tell you of the good folks who share their home with me,
And I don't want to fail them—they think I'm brave, you see—
So I can't let them see me cry; 'twould only make them sad;
But this is my first Christmas without my mom and dad."

With trembling lips and eyes so dimmed by tears he could not see,
He there collapsed and cried and cried beside the Christmas tree.
Now here's a fact most folks don't know: each year on Christmas Day,
God grants that little trees can talk if they have things to say.

And so it was, this little tree, so touched by what it heard,
Tossed wildly by the icy winds, looked down and said these words,
"Please, dry your tears and talk to me, for I am lonely, too.
Together we can chase the clouds and bring back skies of blue."

Well, that was how it started, and they talked most all day long.
And lo! the shades of sadness were dimmed and almost gone.
The tree spoke words of wisdom, bringing comfort to the boy,
And told him of God's Heaven where his parents knew great joy

And that someday he'd be summoned to join them round the Throne
In a place where there's no sorrow and parting is not known,
Where young folks stay forever young and grandmas age no more;
And so 'twill be eternally beyond God's golden door.

By now the shades of eventide were settling o'er the snow;
The colored lights of Christmas lit the village far below.
A smile was on the orphan's face, and though one lingering tear
Slid down his cheek, his eyes revealed he'd vanished every fear.

Years fled; he grew from boy to man, from blonde to ancient gray,
And with each year, he cherished more the memory of that day.
But at times he wonders if things were as they seemed,
Or if, in his deep sorrow, he fell asleep and dreamed.

Sounds
of Christmas

Sounds of Christmas now begin to fall about our ear;
In the distance steeple bells are ringing loud and clear.
Children's laughter can be heard in the frosty air,
People shuffling in the streets, excitement everywhere.
Youngsters whispering secrets of gifts they'd like to find
Under the tree from good Saint Nick, ever generous and kind.
The sound of tinkling sleigh bells has a lilting flair,
Muffling the caroling voices of crescendos debonair.
Snowflakes descending softly, forerunners of Christmastide,
Pile powdery fluff on rooftops with a nonchalance of pride.
Felling of firs in woodlands vibrates the frosty ground,
To be gathered up in bundles, amidst their crackling sound.
The fireplace has sputtering logs, fusing a soft amber light,
Weaving a spell of enchantment this season of mystic delight.
Embrace the sounds of Christmas, with memories old and new;
Toast the clatter of Yuletide, and happiness will pursue.

Ann Schneider

A Song at Christmas

Sing a merry song at Christmas of Santa and his toys,
Of dolls and sleds and storybooks for waiting girls and boys,
Of holly wreaths in windows and trees with tinsel gay,
Of mistletoe and laughter, sleigh bells jingling far away.

Sing a joyful song at Christmas of praises to the King,
The Baby in the manger who came peace and joy to bring,
Of the shepherds and the Wise Men from eastern lands afar
Who, bearing gifts to Bethlehem, were guided by a star.

Sing a song of love at Christmas, love for our fellowmen;
Let that love be our offering to the Babe of Bethlehem.
Then will the peace and joy of that first glad Christmas song
Be echoed in our hearts and lives, every day the whole year long.

Annie M. Israel

Christmas Music

I love the music for Christmas Day,
Carols sung in the same old way,
Voices of old and those so young,
Christmas Carols from every tongue.

Oh, for the music of Christmas Day,
Bringing the greatest joy
To every tiny little girl,
To every growing boy.

Music soft and sweet and clear,
Echoing from the voices here,
Filling air with music bright,
Music sung on a Christmas night.

Cynthia Holt Cummings

Christmastime

Soft feathery flakes of snow adorn
The waxy green of cedar bough;
White icing covers stubble fields
And furrows from last summer's plow.

The frozen pond's a counterpane
Swept clean by cold wind blowing free
Where rabbits play and leave for day
Their moonlight-woven filigree.

The rafters ring with songs of cheer;
A Christmas tree is trimmed and tall,
The family sheltered snug inside,
A rosy glow of love for all.

The hall is stacked with ribboned gifts;
Our hearts are filled with hope sublime
Of peace on earth, good will to men,
A gift of God at Christmastime.

Dan A. Hoover

Keeping Christmas

Let the star shine in your window;
Let the Christ come through your door,
And the hopes and joys of Christmas
Will be yours forevermore.

As it shone for seer and shepherd,
So the star still shines for you
In its bright and ancient splendor,
Keeping Christmas ever new.

To keep Christmas—here's the secret
Which I gladly shall impart—
Keep the starlight in your window
And the Christ Child in your heart.

Minnie Klemme

For You, All the Bright and the Merry

And now is the season of Christmas,
The merriest time of the year,
When the frosty air rings
With the message it brings—
May your days glow with laughter and cheer.

May each hand that you clasp be in friendship
And the smile on each face be for you.
Like the lights on the tree,
May your happiness be
Ever gay, ever bright, ever new.

May each lamp be a beacon of welcome
And each door open wide at your touch.
Swift as snowflakes that fly,
May the joys multiply
For you who have given so much.

May your day, like the tinsel, be shining,
Golden hours in a sparkling string,
And when Christmas is through,
May its memory, for you,
Be a bright and a shimmering thing.

Mary Turton Johnson

Christmas Is

Christmas is the rustle of secrets,
Tinsel shining in eyes,
Lighted trees gleaming through warm windows,
Whisperings, surprise.

It's stockings hung beside gay chimneys,
The silvery peal of bells,
Candy canes and midnight carols,
Kitchens with spicy smells.

Christmas is the Christ Child's birthday.
It's love's own counterpart,
Neighbors running in to borrow,
Chimes tinkling in your heart.

It is the fine, large giving
Of little, big-stitched gifts;
It's Santa Clauses in red flannel,
Moonglow on snowdrifts,

Holly berries bursting from corners,
The woodsy scent of pine.
It is the soul's immortal music;
It is the heart's star-shine!

Emily Carey Alleman

Saint Nicholas's First Trip

Many years ago in a little town far away, there lived a happy, jolly little man named Nicholas. He was born in Patros, a city in Asia Minor, about three hundred years after the birth of Jesus. Nicholas devoted his time to studying the Bible, and he became known as Saint Nicholas. There are many legends told of this plump little man dressed in red. He was a happy man, and he loved to share his good fortune with others, especially the poor.

Now in this same little town where Saint Nicholas was living, there lived three very sad and lonely sisters. They were very poor and had no family except for themselves. They were unhappy because they had no husbands. Now back in those days, in order for a lady to find a husband, she must first have a dowry, which was money, property, or something of value to offer the young man. Tilda, Martha, and Jane had nothing. Saint Nicholas had learned of their problem, but he didn't know what to do about it. So Saint Nicholas wondered to himself, "What must I do?"

One night in the dead of winter it was snowing, and Saint Nicholas couldn't sleep. He put on his warm clothes and started for a walk. The air was cold and brisk, and the snow was falling softly. It was very quiet outside, and all that could be heard was the crunch of the snow under his boots as he trudged on. Soon Saint Nicholas found himself standing in front of the three sisters' house, and as he looked at it he was still wondering, "What can I do?"

Now in those days, poor girls were lucky if they owned more than one pair of stockings. So each night they would wash their stockings and hang them over the fireplace to dry. Through the candle-lit window, he could see the sisters as they hung their stockings by the fire to dry. At this very moment an idea was born. "I know, I know what I'm going to do," he thought. "I'll put gold in their stockings." So with this thought, he hurried home to get that treasure.

Later on that night when Saint Nicholas thought the girls were asleep, he started back to their house. The snow had stopped falling now and the moon was shining brightly and the stars twinkled like diamonds in the sky. The whole countryside was a white, beautiful, peaceful, and happy picture. When he arrived at the house, he quietly slipped inside and without making a sound, he put a handful of sparkling gold into each girl's stocking. Wearing a big smile, he went back out into the magic night and headed for home. The next morning when Tilda, Martha, and Jane found the gold, they were so happy they danced for joy. They each found a nice husband and were very happy. And as for Saint Nicholas—he was very happy too.

From that day on, every year about this time, his memory comes into homes all over the world as stories are told and stockings are filled and good cheer is brought to all, both young and old.

Sara K. Blankenship

A Christmas Gift

Once upon a Christmas Eve many years ago,
A little girl stood misty eyed and watched the falling snow.
Her clothes were tattered and quite worn; her hands were very cold;
She had no toys, just one small doll, and that was very old.
Her only friend was her little dog who never left her side;
He was her pal and playmate, and he cheered her when she cried.
She had no parents; they had left when she was very small,
And other than her old grandmom, she had no one at all.
So Christmas was a lonely time—no gifts, no tree, no lights;
In fact, the crackling fireplace was her only joy that night.
And as she sat by the fireside and watched the roaring flame,
She daydreamed of the things she wished that never, ever came.
She dreamed of Christmas dinners and stockings filled with toys;
She dreamed of family parties with laughter, songs, and noise.
She thought of pretty presents that loved ones gave each other,
And she softly prayed for one small gift to give her dear grandmother.
And although she knew that miracles were very, very rare,
She hoped that someone, somewhere, would hear her quiet prayer.
And as the night passed slowly by and the firelight grew dim,
She kissed her sleeping grandmom and hummed a Christmas hymn.
Then she curled up with her little dog on a musty, pillowed chair,
Protected by an old patch-quilt from the chilly nighttime air.
And as her eyelids slowly closed, suddenly it seemed
That someone there was watching her, and it wasn't just a dream.
She saw a man all dressed in red with a beard as white as snow.
He was quite short and rather plump, and he seemed to softly glow.
He stood there in the darkened room and lightly touched her hair,
And then he gently patted her dog sleeping in the chair.
Then quietly he bent over her and whispered in her ear,
And what she heard just stirred her heart and caused her eyes to tear.
"I've traveled far, my little one, to be with you tonight,
And because you are my final stop, my bag is very light.
So I have not brought you clothes or food or boxes full of toys,
But I've brought an end to sadness and a future full of joys.
My gift to you is growing up with family and with friends,
And a life of love and happiness that will never, ever end.
And when your dear grandchildren come, at one time or another,
Their gift to you will be the love you've given your grandmother."
And she knew this was her miracle and the answer to her prayer;
Then he wished her Merry Christmas and vanished in the air.
And when the sun of Christmas Morning brought a bright new day,
The little girl knelt on her knees and again began to pray.
But now she didn't ask for gifts or a tree of sparkling light;
Her prayer was thanks for the gift of love she got that Christmas night.

Dr. Donald R. Stoltz
President
Norman Rockwell Museum
Philadelphia, Pa.

Christmas Tapestry

Special Thoughts About Christmas

Christmas,
like a hearth fire
remembered in night's chill,
draws the wanderers by heartstrings
back home.

Virginia Blanck Moore

The Christmas lamp is burning
As it did once long ago;
And friendship's light is glowing
Across earth-hiding snow.
The Christmas lamp is bringing
Peace from heaven above
And messages from God, himself,
To absent ones we love.

Mary Wheeler Edgerton

The star shines on
For those with eyes to see,
A finite gleam
Toward all infinity.

Eleanor A. E. Chaffee

For every Christmas candle
That glows on Christmas night
May some gladness come to you
To make your Christmas bright,
And may the pleasant memories
Of this joyous season last
To cheer your heart long after
Its happy hours are past.

Author Unknown

A calmness sweet and most complete
Spreads over all the earth.
The joy it brings, when angels sing,
Announces the Christ Child's birth.
The star that shone that holy night,
Still in the East is seen
To guide and guard the traveler on
By its most radiant beam.
"Peace on earth, good will toward men!"
Let joy triumphant ring,
And may the brotherhood of man
Proclaim Him Christ, our King.

J. Evans Anderson

May you have
The gladness of Christmas
Which is Hope,
The spirit of Christmas
Which is Peace,
The heart of Christmas
Which is Love.

Author Unknown

The rounded cheeks of Earth are bright
With a holly-glow,
And she has tucked a sprig of green
In her hair of snow—
Mistletoe, so not to miss
Thrill of Merry-Christmas kiss.

June Masters Bacher

I heard the bells
On Christmas Day
Their old familiar
Carols play;
And mild and sweet
The words repeat
Of peace on earth,
Good will to men.

Henry Wadsworth Longfellow

The gleam within a childish eye,
Friendliness in passersby,
The word that makes someone rejoice
And softness in a well-known voice,
Good will spirit in the heart,
The star that set this time apart,
An extra meaning in the day,
The Baby in the scent of hay—
These all are Christmas.

Jane Sloan

What do I want for Christmas?
Give me a gift of snow,
A fairyland of winter-white
Beyond the firelight's glow,
A postcard type of beauty
For worlds of gay delight!
This, I want most for Christmas—
Deep snowfall in the night!

Louise Weibert Sutton

Untie the ribbons,
Open with care;
In bright colored boxes
Are gifts rich and rare.

Health, wealth, and laughter,
Love lighting the way
To faith in His teaching
On this Christmas Day.

Ursula Toomey

Let's dance and sing and make good cheer,
For Christmas comes but once a year.

G. MacFarren

On Christmas Day,
There is an
Unseen gift
Each of us
Can give
To the other:

Let us give a secret promise,
To last from this Christmas
To the next,

To share
The frankincense of joy,
The myrrh of kindness,
The silver and gold
Of friendship.

Alberta Dredla

May Christmas peace
Fill all the land
With children walking
Hand in hand,
And may the joy
Of Christmas light
Sparkle in their eyes
Tonight.

Cynthia Holt Cummings

Potpourri

Patchwork quilts
A cozy fire
Homemade cookies
A caroling choir
Frosty windows
A snow-covered lane
Quaint covered bridges
And sweet candy canes
Pine-bough wreaths
And bayberry candles
Toy soldiers
And stockings hung
On the mantel
The fragrance of pine
A garland of holly
Red velvet ribbons
And Santa so jolly
Gaily wrapped gifts
And greetings
Of good cheer
The ringing of sleigh bells—
Christmas is here!

Nancy L. Kratowicz

With Love

"We'll be looking for you both
Quite early Christmas Eve,"
The letter signed "with love,"
A phrase not hard to believe.
Then thoughts raced out
Across the starry sky's great bend
To Christmas Eve and love that waits
At Christmas journey's end.

Within the family circle
On this quiet holy night,
Love dwells in eyes that shine
With tender, pure delight;
And young and old come closer to
The deeper meaning of
That Christmas Eve, so long ago,
That sent God's gift of love.

For Christmastime is family time
The whole wide world around,
And in the earthbound heart of man
No greater love is found
When Christmas Eve lights candles
That catch The Star's own light,
To glow in hearts throughout the years
"With love," forever bright.

Willard G. Seaman

The Heart Goes Home

The heart goes home on Christmas Day.
Though you're a million miles away,
There comes the time your heart will leave
To span all space on Christmas Eve
And walk a path across a hill,
Where candles burn on a windowsill,
To find in old remembered places
Love and welcome on dear faces.
Yes, the lonely heart will find its way,
And if even all have gone away,
Love is there, secure and strong.
This a heart will find and long
For home again, however far,
Along the way of the Christmas star.

Lucille McBroom Crumley

Christmas Excitement

Ornaments and tinsel,
Glowing lights on shapely trees,
Indoor decorations
And wreaths and trim to please,

Gatherings of neighbors
And of relatives and friends,
Special preparations
While warmth of song transcends,

Christmas punch and fruitcakes,
Bright wrappings, gifts and toys,
Excitement and elation
In hearts of girls and boys—

We're ready for a birthday,
And our homes are at their best.
Dear God, help us prepare our hearts
For You, the honored Guest.

Author Unknown

Days of Christmas

The shopping is over,
The rushing is done,
The tree is a picture,
And now we have fun!
When friends come a-calling
For holiday brunch,
We bring out the fruitcake,
The cookies, and punch.
We read all the greetings
So carefully signed
And find in each message
A heart that is kind.
But oh, we are happy—
The rushing is done.
The days around Christmas
Are peaceful … and fun.

Hilda Butler Farr

Now
Is the Time

Now is the time of Christmas,
So new and yet so old.
Both Micah and Isaiah
The Savior's birth foretold.
Saint Matthew told of Wise Men
Who brought gifts to their King.
Luke told of humble shepherds
Who heard God's angels sing.

All these are part of Christmas,
The wreath upon the door,
A million stars appearing
To bless each church and store.
The holly and the ivy
Climb up the front-hall stair
While mincemeat pies and crumb cakes
Spread fragrance everywhere.

These are the signs of Christmas;
The world begins to change.
From door to door rank strangers
Have greetings to exchange.
The bells ring out His glory;
Sweet songs acclaim His birth.
The story of the Christ Child
Resounds throughout the earth.

Alice Leedy Mason

Merry Christmas

When Christmas bells chime far and near
And silver-bright the tall stars stand,
When thin and sweet the echoes drift
From carols all across the land,
It is a time for hearts to turn
The pages of remembering

With all their bits of cherished trove—
A smile, a touch, a tinseled string,
Some verses on a faded card,
A shining moment, misty far
As silver echoes of a bell,
Or radiance of a distant star;
A time when, heartened by the glow
That such remembering imparts,
Once more, through dear familiar words,
To keep Noel with kindred hearts.

Jessie Wilmore Murton

The Finest Gift

At Christmastime a special gift
Is not upon the tree;
It is never tied with ribbons,
Nor is it something one can see.

Yet among all the lights so bright
And presents wrapped and gay,
It is the finest gift of all
For every Christmas Day.

It is the love of Christmastime
Aglow in every heart,
All the good will of the season
In which all may have part.

Virginia Katherine Oliver

Bright Star

Christmas holly, Christmas trees,
Gift wraps gay and bright,
Wonderment in shining eyes
Makes a Christmas right.
Reading in the treasured book
Of the hallowed birth,
Caroling and greetings sent,
Prayers for peace on earth,
Christmas holds a deepening
Of life for everyone;
How precious must our Father hold
This birthday of His Son.

Irene Taylor

In 1818, Joseph Mohr
Wrote the unforgettable words,
"Silent Night" (Stille Nacht),
To the enchanting music
By Franz Gruber.

For many generations,
Men, women, and children
Of all nations
Have sung and continue to sing
This cherished Christmas carol.

Words of simplicity and beauty
Should not be consumed in one breath,
But should be sipped and relished;
For the flavor of these words,
Like vintage wine, should be savored and enjoyed.

"The Miracle of 'Silent Night'" contains
Meditations born of the lines
In the three verses of Joseph Mohr's "Silent Night."
May these meditations remain in your heart
Each Christmas and in all the days in between.

The Miracle of Silent Night

Silent Night, Holy Night

A starlit night of holiness and awe.
A glimmer of eternal love
Offering a timeless, infinite gift
Of supreme hallowed grace.

All Is Calm, All Is Bright

Prayer is a sea of tranquillity,
A tide of serenity that brings forth
An everlasting calm into our lives.

Holy Infant So Tender and Mild

Our thoughts, words, and deeds
Must be gentle and loving
As if we were thinking of, talking to,
And caring for the Infant Jesus.

Round Yon Virgin Mother and Child

Let us bring our fears, sorrows,
Joys and prayers of gratitude
As we kneel before Mary's Infant Son
In the chapel of our hearts.

Sleep in Heavenly Peace, Sleep in Heavenly Peace.

The peace of the sleeping Infant
Prevails, in holiness and grace,
Remaining with us always
As we live in heavenly peace.

Silent Night, Holy Night

Holiness is a flower
Born of silent courage—
Courage inspired by prayer
And the love of our Heavenly Father.

Shepherds Quake at Thy Sight

A sight to behold! Fear not!
Embrace God's messenger,
The angel of the Lord,
With love, humility, and trust.

Glories Stream from Heaven Afar

The glory of God shines
All about us, wherever we may be,
His illustrious light constantly projected
Upon the screen of life.

Heavenly Hosts Sing Alleluia

Let us sing Alleluia
With the heavenly hierarchy;
Let our joyful voices be heard
By all people of all nations.

Christ the Savior Is Born, Christ the Savior Is Born.

The Redeemer of all God's people,
The Christ Child, is born not only
In the town of Bethlehem
But in each of us.

Silent Night, Holy Night

The glorious brilliance of God's love
Glitters and gleams upon us
Like the star of Bethlehem
On that holy night of old.

Son of God, Love's Pure Light

What greater gift could God send us
Than His Infant Son wrapped
Not only in swaddling clothes,
But in purity, love, and truth?

Radiant Beams from Thy Holy Face

The sacred smile radiating
From the Infant's venerable face
Enlightens our faith with divine love.

With the Dawn of Redeeming Grace

Children of light, awake each dawn
In the splendor of God's holy love
And His sanctifying grace.

Jesus Lord, at Thy Birth, Jesus Lord, at Thy Birth.

Each Christmas, we rejoice
For the Infant Jesus is born.
Each new day, we rejoice
For the Christ Child grows
In wisdom, age, and grace within us.

Dorothy Travers Zisa

The Christmas Story

And it came to pass in those days, that there went out a decree from Caesar Augustus, that all the world should be taxed. (And this taxing was first made when Cyrenius was governor of Syria.) And all went to be taxed, every one into his own city. And Joseph also went up from Galilee, out of the city of Nazareth, into Judea, unto the city of David, which is called Bethlehem; (because he was of the house and lineage of David:) To be taxed with Mary his espoused wife, being great with child. And so it was, that, while they were there, the days were accomplished that she should be delivered. And she brought forth her firstborn son, and wrapped him in swaddling clothes, and laid him in a manger; because there was no room for them in the inn.

Luke 2:1-7

Now when Jesus was born in Bethlehem of Judea in the days of Herod the king, behold, there came wise men from the east to Jerusalem, Saying, Where is he that is born King of the Jews? for we have seen his star in the east, and are come to worship him. When Herod the king had heard these things, he was troubled, and all Jerusalem with him. And when he had gathered all the chief priests and scribes of the people together, he demanded of them where Christ should be born. And they said unto him, In Bethlehem of Judea: for thus it is written by the prophet, And thou Bethlehem, in the land of Juda, art not the least among the princes of Juda: for out of thee shall come a Governor, that shall rule my people Israel. Then Herod, when he had privily called the wise men, inquired of them diligently what time the star appeared. And he sent them to Bethlehem, and said, Go and search diligently for the young child; and when ye have found him, bring me word again, that I may come and worship him also. When they had heard the king, they departed; and, lo, the star, which they saw in the east, went before them, till it came and stood over where the young child was. When they saw the star, they rejoiced with exceeding great joy.

And when they were come into the house, they saw the young child with Mary his mother, and fell down, and worshipped him: and when they had opened their treasures, they presented unto him gifts; gold, and frankincense, and myrrh. And being warned of God in a dream that they should not return to Herod, they departed into their own country another way.

Matthew 2:1-12

And there were in the same country shepherds abiding in the field, keeping watch over their flock by night. And, lo, the angel of the Lord came upon them, and the glory of the Lord shone round about them: and they were sore afraid. And the angel said unto them, Fear not: for, behold, I bring you good tidings of great joy, which shall be to all people. For unto you is born this day in the city of David a Saviour, which is Christ the Lord. And this shall be a sign unto you; Ye shall find the babe wrapped in swaddling clothes, lying in a manger. And suddenly there was with the angel a multitude of the heavenly host praising God, and saying, Glory to God in the highest, and on earth peace, good will toward men. And it came to pass, as the angels were gone away from them into heaven, the shepherds said one to another, Let us now go even unto Bethlehem, and see this thing which is come to pass, which the Lord hath made known unto us. And they came with haste, and found Mary, and Joseph, and the babe lying in a manger. And when they had seen it, they made known abroad the saying which was told them concerning this child. And all they that heard it wondered at those things which were told them by the shepherds. But Mary kept all these things, and pondered them in her heart. And the shepherds returned, glorifying and praising God for all the things that they had heard and seen, as it was told unto them.

Luke 2:8-20

Christmas
Thoughts

Katherine Edelman

How wonderful it would have been
To hear the song, to see the star,
To watch the Wise Men as they came
With gifts and treasure from afar.

But much more wonderful than all,
To stand with love and wondering awe
Beside the Christ Child as He lay
So sweetly small, on bed of straw.

Oh, to Have Been a Shepherd

Dorothy Evelyn Begg

Oh, to have been a shepherd
The night that Christ was born!
To have heard the hallelujahs
And that angelic horn!

To have crossed the plain to Bethlehem
With sandals on my feet;
To have touched the hand of God's own Son
Where He lay upon the wheat!

To have seen the bright heraldic star;
To have found the manger place;
To have seen the cattle kneeling
And Mary's shining face!

Oh, to have been a shepherd
The night that Christ was born;
To have carried in my heart for life
The glory of that dawn!

A Midwife's Dream

Charlotte Partin

If only I'd been living
Two thousand years ago,
I'd have packed my midwife's bag;
To Bethlehem I'd go.

Here is what I'd carry
On that blessed, holy morn;
'Tis what I'd bring for Mary
For when her son was born:

A little robe of linen,
Warm stockings for his feet,
A tiny crown as soft as down
For that precious head so sweet.
For Joseph, I'd make herbal tea
And several loaves of bread.
I'd place two silken pillows
Beneath fair Mary's head.
She'd sit near the stable door
While I combed her lovely hair.
When the shepherds and the Wise Men
Would pay humble homage there,
I'd let them enter,
One by one,
And bid them view, two seconds,
Her peaceful, sleeping son.

They would have been more comfortable
If only I'd been there
With my tattered midwife's bag
So full of love and care.

Such joy it would have brought me—
'Twould cause my heart to sing—
If only it had been my touch
That lulled Christ the King!

The birth of Jesus Christ and the visit of the wise men according to the Gospel of Saint Matthew:

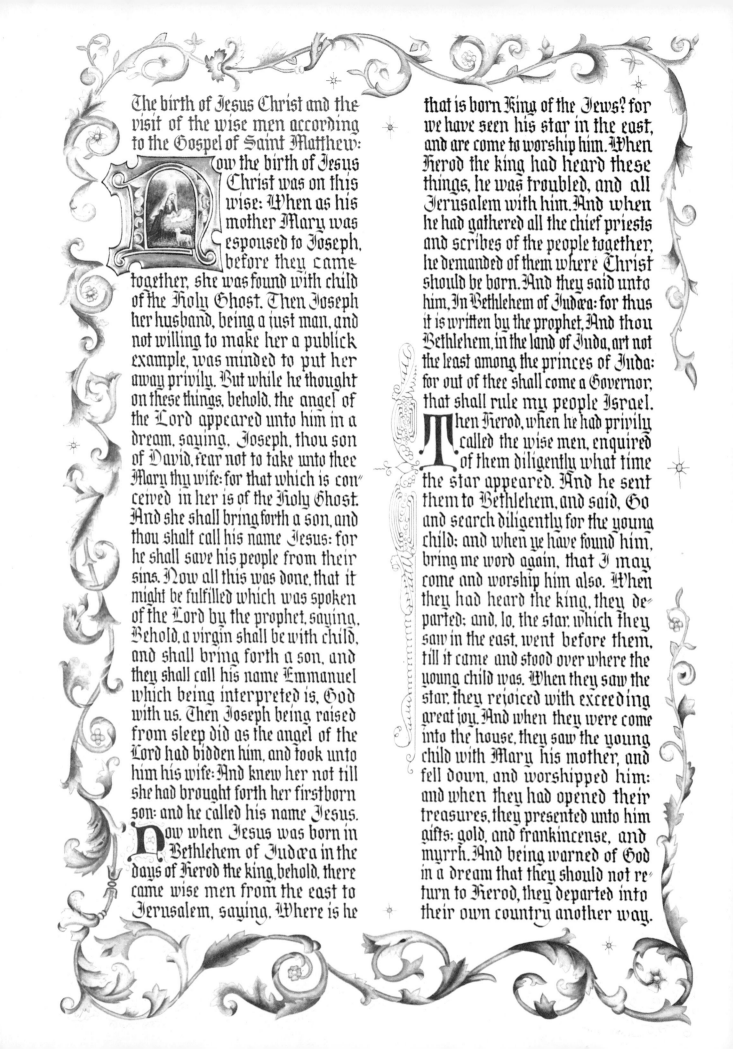

Now the birth of Jesus Christ was on this wise: When as his mother Mary was espoused to Joseph, before they came together, she was found with child of the Holy Ghost. Then Joseph her husband, being a just man, and not willing to make her a publick example, was minded to put her away privily. But while he thought on these things, behold, the angel of the Lord appeared unto him in a dream, saying, Joseph, thou son of David, fear not to take unto thee Mary thy wife: for that which is conceived in her is of the Holy Ghost. And she shall bring forth a son, and thou shalt call his name Jesus: for he shall save his people from their sins. Now all this was done, that it might be fulfilled which was spoken of the Lord by the prophet, saying, Behold, a virgin shall be with child, and shall bring forth a son, and they shall call his name Emmanuel which being interpreted is, God with us. Then Joseph being raised from sleep did as the angel of the Lord had bidden him, and took unto him his wife: And knew her not till she had brought forth her firstborn son: and he called his name Jesus.

Now when Jesus was born in Bethlehem of Judæa in the days of Herod the king, behold, there came wise men from the east to Jerusalem, saying, Where is he that is born King of the Jews? for we have seen his star in the east, and are come to worship him. When Herod the king had heard these things, he was troubled, and all Jerusalem with him. And when he had gathered all the chief priests and scribes of the people together, he demanded of them where Christ should be born. And they said unto him, In Bethlehem of Judæa: for thus it is written by the prophet, And thou Bethlehem, in the land of Juda, art not the least among the princes of Juda: for out of thee shall come a Governor, that shall rule my people Israel.

Then Herod, when he had privily called the wise men, enquired of them diligently what time the star appeared. And he sent them to Bethlehem, and said, Go and search diligently for the young child; and when ye have found him, bring me word again, that I may come and worship him also. When they had heard the king, they departed; and, lo, the star, which they saw in the east, went before them, till it came and stood over where the young child was. When they saw the star, they rejoiced with exceeding great joy. And when they were come into the house, they saw the young child with Mary his mother, and fell down, and worshipped him: and when they had opened their treasures, they presented unto him gifts; gold, and frankincense, and myrrh. And being warned of God in a dream that they should not return to Herod, they departed into their own country another way.

The Christmas Nativity Tradition

Ever since Saint Francis of Assisi celebrated Mass at a specially constructed manger in 1223 at Greccio, Italy, Nativity scenes have been an important part of Christmas celebrations. This tradition spread quickly in both the church and home observations of the season.

By the eighteenth century, building a model crib, or praesepio, had become a popular craft in Naples. The people who made the cribs were known as figuarari, and the figures they produced were named pastori. King Carlo III, fascinated by anything mechanical, built his own lavish Nativity scenes for his castle, and the queen and her ladies-in-waiting made costumes for the figures. Soon elaborate Nativity scenes became very popular at court. At the same time, Fra Gregorio Rocco, a civic crusader, began a campaign to fight crime by urging every family to built its own praesepio.

As time passed and the custom of building Nativity scenes spread through Italy and into Germany, it developed into the construction of entire model towns, villages, and castles containing the manger. Thus the modelers displayed the everyday life of their time with Jesus at the center of it all.

This custom spread from Europe to America and Africa and throughout the world and continues to be a meaningful part of the observance of Christmas.

Anne Dorlon
Cybis

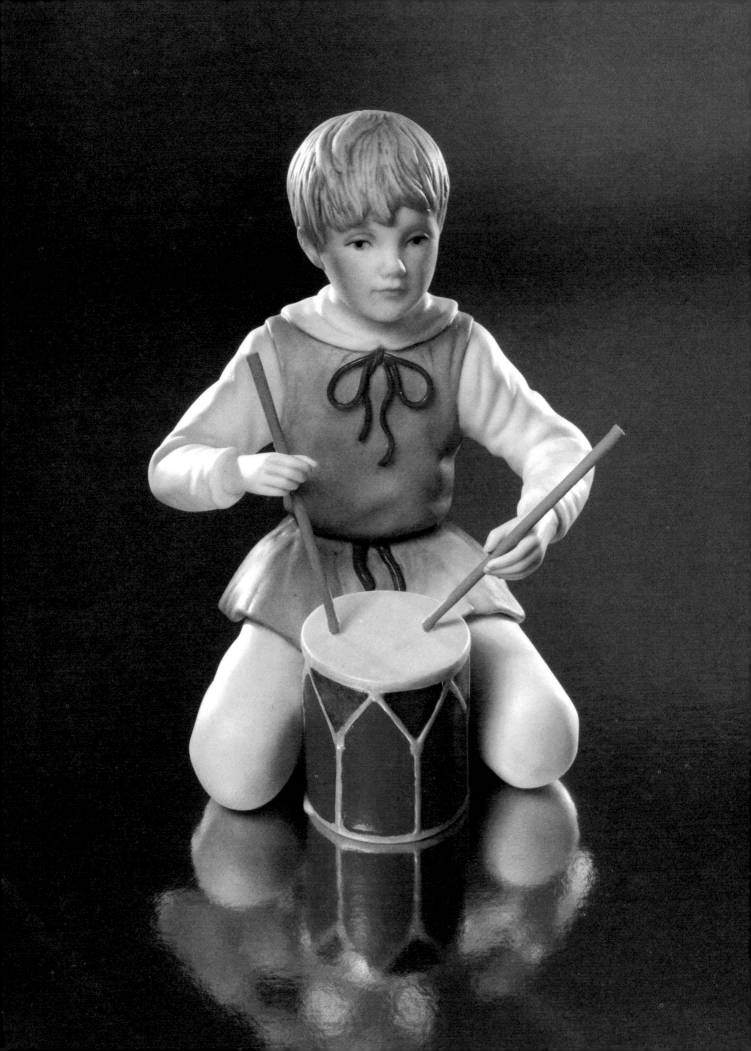

THE LITTLE DRUMMER BOY

Little Baby, Pa-rum-pa-pum-pum,
I am a poor boy too, Pa-rum-pa-pum-pum.
I have no gift to bring, Pa-rum-pa-pum-pum,
That's fit to give our King! Pa-rum-pa-pum-pum.
Rum-pa-pum-pum, rum-pa-pum-pum,
Shall I play for You, Pa-rum-pa-pum-pum,
On my drum?

Mary nodded, Pa-rum-pa-pum-pum.
The ox and lamb kept time, Pa-rum-pa-pum-pum.
I played my drum for Him, Pa-rum-pa-pum-pum,
I played my best for Him, Pa-rum-pa-pum-pum,
Rum-pa-pum-pum, rum-pa-pum-pum.
Then He smiled at me, Pa-rum-pa-pum-pum!
Me and my drum!

Katherine Davis, Henry Onorati and Harry Simeone

THE ABC'S

Angels from the realms of glory,
Telling of the Christmas story.

Bethlehem beckons with joyful accord;
Come hither, come see, and worship the Lord.

Christ was born on Christmas Day,
Asleep in a manger, a bed made of hay.

Divine and holy is Thy birth;
Wing Your flight o'er all the earth.

Everlasting Father, and Father of all,
Look with mercy and love on us all.

"Fear not," said the angel, one night long ago.
"I bring you good tidings, for this I know."

"Glory to the Son," we sing,
"Christ, our Prophet, Priest and King."

Heavenly hosts, their watch are keeping,
Precious child so sweetly sleeping.

Immanuel, we sing Thy praise,
Thou Prince of Life, Thou Fount of Grace.

Joy to the world, the Lord is come,
Born in a manger, God's only son.

King of Kings, prophets foretold,
Now all men His love behold.

Love is a gift He gives to all,
To each of us, both great and small.

Messiah and Savior—for this He came—
Live in our hearts and there remain.

OF CHRISTMAS

Night so holy, silent and still,
Proclaiming joy, peace and good will.

Odors of Edom and offerings divine,
Myrrh from the forest and gold from the mine.

Peace on earth, good will from heaven,
Souls redeemed and sins forgiven.

Quietly He came to earth
To give us all a second birth.

Rejoice, give thanks and loudly sing,
Glory to the new-born King.

Shepherds watched their flocks by night
While Wise Men followed the heavenly light.

Tidings of great joy I bring;
Good news from heaven the angels sing.

Unto us a child is born
On this happy Christmas Morn.

Virgin-born, Immanuel,
Let every tongue Thy praises tell.

Wise Men from the East, they came
To worship and praise His holy name.

X is for Christ when in Greek it is read;
A Savior, the Lord, so the angel said.

Yonder shines brightly the heavenly star
Showing the way to those from afar.

Zeal was bestowed on God's only Son
From His childhood years till His work was done.

Jeanne Blomquest

Christmas is a fairyland
Of scented candles' glow,
Of winged angels and bright stars,
Holly and mistletoe,

Of gingerbread men
And old rag dolls,
Jack-in-the-boxes
And bouncing balls,

Of soldiers that march
And horses that prance,
Of toys that spin
And dolls that dance.

Toys that Santa brings to life
To bring Christmas joy—
They dance and talk and delight
Every girl and boy.

Christmas is a fairyland
Where wishes can come true,
For underneath the Christmas tree
Surprises await you.

Yes, Christmas is a fairyland
Of trees aglow with light;
Hung with balls and candy canes,
They twinkle in the night!

Christmas Is a Fairyland!

Nancy Jean Conley

Christmas Toys

A little dappled horse, a scarlet ball,
A woolly lamb, a doll with sleepy eyes,
A small white angel for a Christmas tree,
A Christmas stocking with a bulky prize.

Red mittens on a string, a pair of skates,
A toy balloon to drift above the house,
Tinsel to glisten in the candlelight,
A little scarlet-coated Mickey Mouse.

A set of dishes for a little girl
With tiny brier roses here and there,
A locket on a little golden chain,
New patent leather shoes for her to wear.

O crisp December, gay with mistletoe,
Holly and cedar hanging on the door,
Old folks to love, carols to sing in church,
And little children to buy presents for.

Edna Jaques

The Wonder of a Christmas Night

In folds of white the newly fallen snow
Carpets quiet streets in glistening mounds.
As distant church lights cast an amber glow,
A deep-toned bell across the whiteness sounds
The evening call to worship. Now hurried throngs
Unite to honor His Nativity,
And carolers' voices ring with treasured songs,
All symbols of this day's reality.

As evening deepens, snowbanks catch the light.
New stars wink, each one a diamond spark
As peace and love transform the Christmas night
With faith and hope to lift us from the dark.
The wonder of belief shall give us reason
To praise the Christ Child's birth this joyous season.

Ruby Waters Erdelen

December Night

December night! when myriad stars are shining
And all the world seems dressed in dazzling white,
There glows a beauty that has no defining
Throughout the splendor of the silent night.

Celestial night! beyond this finite glory
We offer homage to a Star so bright
It brings our world life's most enchanting story,
The tender ministry of Holy Night.

George Nicholas Rees

Little choral groups singing carols gay,
Heralds of glad tidings on the way,
Homes arrayed in multicolored lights
Add beauty galore to star-studded nights.

Hometown Christmas Eve

A scent of pine fills cool crisp air;
Smiling faces grace lighted windows everywhere.
The whole town radiates with homey bliss;
God grant it shall always be like this.

Peace and tranquillity so profound
Echo the friendly voices' greetings sound—
A MERRY CHRISTMAS to all in sight,
The old hometown, Christmas Eve night.

Joseph L. Derbyshire

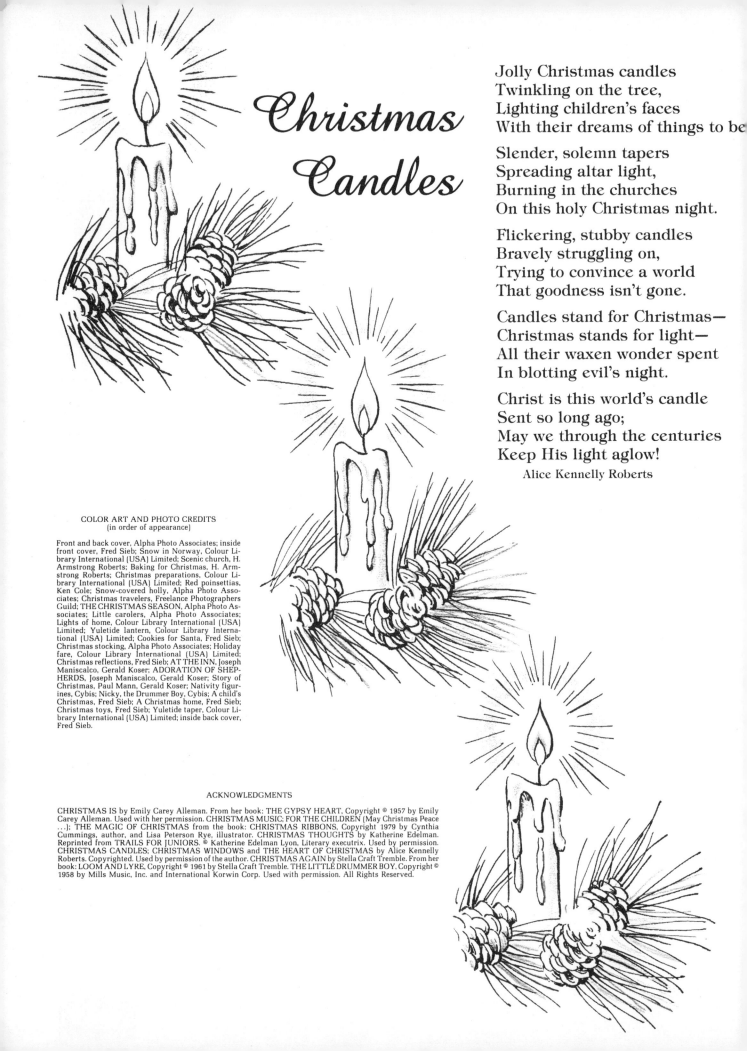

Christmas Candles

Jolly Christmas candles
Twinkling on the tree,
Lighting children's faces
With their dreams of things to be.

Slender, solemn tapers
Spreading altar light,
Burning in the churches
On this holy Christmas night.

Flickering, stubby candles
Bravely struggling on,
Trying to convince a world
That goodness isn't gone.

Candles stand for Christmas—
Christmas stands for light—
All their waxen wonder spent
In blotting evil's night.

Christ is this world's candle
Sent so long ago;
May we through the centuries
Keep His light aglow!

Alice Kennelly Roberts

COLOR ART AND PHOTO CREDITS
(in order of appearance)

Front and back cover, Alpha Photo Associates; inside front cover, Fred Sieb; Snow in Norway, Colour Library International (USA) Limited; Scenic church, H. Armstrong Roberts; Baking for Christmas, H. Armstrong Roberts; Christmas preparations, Colour Library International (USA) Limited; Red poinsettias, Ken Cole; Snow-covered holly, Alpha Photo Associates; Christmas travelers, Freelance Photographers Guild; THE CHRISTMAS SEASON, Alpha Photo Associates; Little carolers, Alpha Photo Associates; Lights of home, Colour Library International (USA) Limited; Yuletide lantern, Colour Library International (USA) Limited; Cookies for Santa, Fred Sieb; Christmas stocking, Alpha Photo Associates; Holiday fare, Colour Library International (USA) Limited; Christmas reflections, Fred Sieb; AT THE INN, Joseph Maniscalco, Gerald Koser; ADORATION OF SHEPHERDS, Joseph Maniscalco, Gerald Koser; Story of Christmas, Paul Mann, Gerald Koser; Nativity figurines, Cybis; Nicky, the Drummer Boy, Cybis; A child's Christmas, Fred Sieb; A Christmas home, Fred Sieb; Christmas toys, Fred Sieb; Yuletide taper, Colour Library International (USA) Limited; inside back cover, Fred Sieb.

ACKNOWLEDGMENTS

CHRISTMAS IS by Emily Carey Alleman. From her book: THE GYPSY HEART, Copyright © 1957 by Emily Carey Alleman. Used with her permission. CHRISTMAS MUSIC; FOR THE CHILDREN (May Christmas Peace ...); THE MAGIC OF CHRISTMAS from the book: CHRISTMAS RIBBONS, Copyright 1979 by Cynthia Cummings, author, and Lisa Peterson Rye, illustrator. CHRISTMAS THOUGHTS by Katherine Edelman. Reprinted from TRAILS FOR JUNIORS. © Katherine Edelman Lyon, Literary executrix. Used by permission. CHRISTMAS CANDLES; CHRISTMAS WINDOWS and THE HEART OF CHRISTMAS by Alice Kennelly Roberts. Copyrighted. Used by permission of the author. CHRISTMAS AGAIN by Stella Craft Tremble. From her book: LOOM AND LYRE, Copyright © 1961 by Stella Craft Tremble. THE LITTLE DRUMMER BOY, Copyright © 1958 by Mills Music, Inc. and International Korwin Corp. Used with permission. All Rights Reserved.

Merry Christmas and a Happy New Year . . .

We at Ideals would like to take this opportunity to express our sincere wishes for a Blessed Holiday Season.

We trust that the beauty and innocence of the child within each of us can again be realized in this country and the world we live in.

We will continue to offer you the quality you have come to expect in each upcoming edition of Ideals.

We look forward to sharing 1983 with you and yours. May the peace of the season continue with you throughout the coming year.